THE CHOCOLATE ORGY has erupted in the world of dating, shaking up controversy with every Princess and Prince! Whether you are a serial dater, or just always seem to strike out, *The Chocolate Orgy*, is A DATING GUIDE TO COOKING UP BITTERSWEET ENDINGS.

With this *Dating Guide*, get ready to finally toss out those boring, cold starters and begin to finally cook up *Desire* with fresh warm appetizers! Each *Chocolate Episode* will have you thrusting forward with new ingredients that make *Cooking up Bittersweet Endings Orgasmic!* The Chocolate Orgy is going to heat up your *Sizzle* and add *Exotic* Flavor to your Spice, beyond the traditional recipes of Love when it comes to *Cooking up Bittersweet Endings*. As you begin to taste this *Dating Guide*, each *Chocolate Episode* will taste more *Orgasmic* than the next. You will also begin to Cook up your own Recipes of Passion, Love, and *Desire* when it comes to Heating up the temperature of Romance, beyond the board—the chopping board!

First Published by
THE ZEN FOOD™ BRAND LLC
Delray Beach, Florida
www.zenfoodplan.com
instagram.com/onceuponazen

This is book two in The Food Orgy™ Series of Books

Story Theme photos by Andres Patino *instagram.com/andresfpatino_photo/*
Unless credited below, food photos and all styling by Michelle Lynn
3D TV image from Freepik
Other photos from Unsplash

Printed in the United States of America

Book design and production assistance from Good Book Developers
www.goodbookdevelopers.com

10 9 8 7 6 5 4 3 2 1

THE CHOCOLATE ORGY

A Dating Guide to Cooking Up

Bittersweet Endings

MICHELLE LYNN

Sit back, relax, and enjoy this dating guide, savoring the sizzling flavor in each episode that leads you to the delicious season finale: The Dessert Fantasy !!!

Episodes

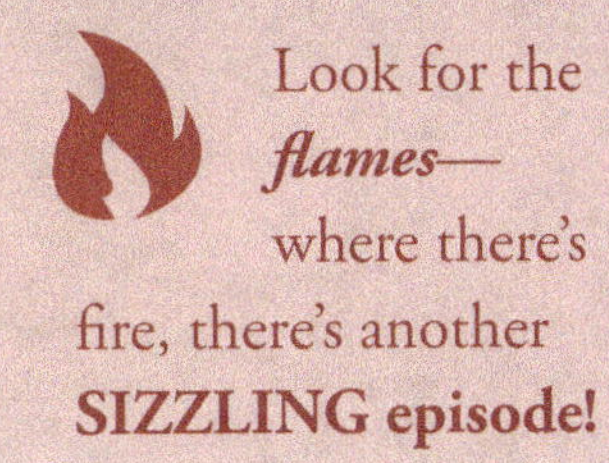

Look for the
flames—
where there's
fire, there's another
SIZZLING episode!

THE CHOCOLATE
ORGY

DEDICATION

I want to dedicate this book to the spiritual world of our ancestors. To my sister Laurie Beth Taubman who had a heart of Gold and a love for Dark Chocolate, and my beloved Grandmother Marylin Taubman, who inspired me through her Sunday family dinners to explore the field of culinary art. God Bless their souls, and to anyone who has lost someone they loved: may they rest in peace.

The New Chapter

From afar, the
Streets looked like
A Washed up dream with
Old Structures that no
longer roofed
Inspiration.

Inside her dream, the
Blue Skies painted a
Brighter Picture with a
New address.
You can tell the way
She arrived, her dream
No longer marked
An unclear destination, but
Became a Roadmap to
Purpose, beyond
The narrow view.

You can tell her dream,
Unwrapped a gift, as she
Began to magically write
The New Chapter

FOREWORD

This page is in honor of the divine spirit that often times is asleep and just needs to be reawakened. This poem was written to inspire you to gain strength to write a New Storyline, one that speaks real character, grace and strength, so continuing to turn over those harder pages become easier. Read this poem to remind you that no matter what chapter you are stuck on, there are always newer chapters awaiting you on your Journey…

INTRODUCTION

The sweet drama ensued from the Naked truth on licking, biting, and swallowing *The Food Orgy* has cooked up a spicier drama, one full of bolder and more intoxicating flavor that operates on a forbidden *Desire* for a darker *Bittersweet Ending*, one called *The Chocolate Orgy!*

The Chocolate Orgy is going to whip, beat, roast, spice, and sweeten the hell out of your Love life when it comes to *Cooking up Bittersweet Endings!* Get ready to finally cook up real flavor in the bland world of *Dating,* so *Bittersweet Endings* can lead to Fantasy! The mysterious *Chocolate* flavor unveiled in each *Chocolate Episode* can finally satisfy a real taste of hunger amongst a dying appetite of Love. Each *Chocolate Episode* is going to melt your icy cold dates into warm mouthwatering moments that cascade down a Waterfall of *Lust,* so *Cooking up The Bittersweet Ending* can finally come into a screaming "*I Love you!*"

CHOCOLATE EPISODE #1

The Chocolate Appetite

The Chocolate Orgy has melted more icy dates on record, ultimately creating a Heat wave of Love, stirring up hunger for a one of a kind Date, A *Chocolate* Date! The *Chocolate* Date can only be kept fresh by continuing to add a Fresh flavor in each *Episode* where Cooking up a Spicy *Passion* with Real Ingredients of Love will keep the flavor Euphoric between you and your Honey when it comes *to Cooking up Bittersweet Endings*!

To increase *The Chocolate Appetite* in this episode, you must come to find out what excites your date's appetite for Love! To cook up the perfect flavor of Love when it comes to stimulating a *Chocolate Appetite*, it boils down to understanding the flavors of passion that melt cold starters!

A *hot* date will always leave you breathless for just one more mouthful! Nevertheless, *The Chocolate Appetite* will enhance your mouthfuls to a whole new level of Spiciness when it comes to *Cooking up Bittersweet Endings*! The conquest to satisfying your date's *Chocolate Appetite* may initially be difficult to get down with, however if you get adventurous to exploring the Flavor of *Desire* you will understand their *Chocolate Appetite.*

Does your Mr. *Sizzle* or Ms. Spice prefer licks and nibbles over mouthfuls, or do they just open their mouth wide to Exotic flavors over traditional ones? The answer to discovering the flavor that satisfies *The Chocolate Appetite* is in the Kama sutra to *Cooking up Bittersweet Endings!*

TOP TIPS IN THE KAMA SUTRA TO
Cooking Up Bittersweet Endings!

TIP #1 PLAY THE SEXY ROLE OF DETECTIVE

The dates that *Sizzle* over *Fizzle* are the ones where you play the role of Detective! This doesn't necessarily mean you have a free pass to cyber stalk Mr. Steamy or Ms. *Sizzle*, but more along the lines of conversation, #s, and research! Just remember to cover your basics with slick questions during conversation and taking note of details regarding their personality, whether it's mild, spicier, or sweet! Also, discover their taste palette by understanding if they prefer to dip into a sweeter night over a spicier night!

TIP #2 FEED EACH OTHER OYSTERS

Oysters, are a strong stimulator of a *Chocolate Appetite*! As far back as the Roman Gods of *Cleopatra*, oysters were known as the "love drug," improving dopamine levels in both men and women, ultimately boosting libido. When in doubt, go for the oysters and leave the silverware behind!

TIP #3 MAKE THEM GO BANANAS

The best way to create a mouthwatering moment is to leave your date going Bananas for more! Bananas are a powerful aphrodisiac when it comes to the game of Love and *Desire*! Bananas contain the bromelain enzyme that increases libido and reverses impotence in men. They are also a game changer in reversing a dry *Chocolate Appetite* to one of a cascading Waterfall of *Lust*! Whether you are cooking up love or dining out, always order up a storm of banana dishes!

TIP #4 COOK UP A SEXY SCENT

Can you cook up a SEXY Scent? The answer is yes!, and it lies right in your kitchen cupboard and garden! Vanilla, *Chocolate*, cinnamon, citrus, licorice, pumpkin pie, buttery popcorn, almond, basil, ginger, sandalwood, patchouli, jasmine, rose, white lily, peppermint, and lavender are the top scents to increasing *The Chocolate Appetite*! Next time, instead of shopping for store scents, get freaky with cooking up a SEXY smell!

TIP #5 DISPLAY A SEXY PRESENTATION

Get into a SEXY Display with your Flavor by dressing up your presentation with final touches that increase your date's Hunger for you! For example, if you're a female, focus on jewelry like chokers or dangling earrings, low cut shirts, sexy heels or skinny jeans. On the other hand if you're a male, focus on wearing masculine pieces like a nice button down, white t-shirt, sexy cologne, a little shadow from not shaving, and grooming. The SEXIER your flavor of love is, the hungrier your date will be when it comes to dessert!

CONCLUSION

By now you are on your way to becoming a XXX performer of *The Chocolate Orgy* so Cooking Up Bittersweet Endings leads to a rock star Fantasy! The Chocolate Appetite mastered in this chapter is a game changer when it comes to perfecting the role of The Chocolate Flirt…

A tale of
Two lovers
Chasing nightfall and
Trailing behind the
Dark shadow of broken
Promises.

You can tell from the
Foggy Romance, her soul
Wandered aimlessly, seeking
Clarity and warm
Expression, yet
His contrasting moments
Became the defining
Masterpiece.

The forgotten shades
Began to wash away
Greys, casting light on
The Portrait of Love,
Painting a magical
Ever after...

21
21A

CHOCOLATE EPISODE #2

The Chocolate Flirt

If the last *Chocolate Episode* didn't leave your date Hungry for more *Chocolate* Romance, then wait until you cook up Passion with *The Chocolate Flirt*!

The main ingredient in this *Chocolate* episode is the HONEY! Without some Love for your HONEY, *The Chocolate Flirt* will not come to life! To make your date fall in Love with the idea of HONEY, you must keep this episode balanced with Real flavor and Sweet Ingredients, so this *Episode* goes down in one *Swallow*! Read on to find out the principles to perfecting *The Chocolate Flirt*.

THE PRINCIPALS TO PERFECTING
The Chocolate Flirt

MAKE EYE CONTACT
Focus on the Pupil of *Lust*.

ACT CONFIDENT
Acting with confidence is going to make coming into the role of *The Chocolate Flirt* that is much easier to Swallow.

CREATE MOUTHWATERING MOMENTS
Concentrate on your date, slow down, and pay attention to those mouthwatering moments and details that keep you attuned with your date.

BECOME PLAYFUL
This applies primarily to physical contact with tiny gestures towards your date which include shoulder touches, hand holding, hugs, kisses on the cheek, and anything that allows you to cook up *The Chocolate Flirt* in a playful manner.

DRESS TO IMPRESS
Wear clothing that screams *Desire*, while also highlighting your best features in *The Chocolate Flirt*!

KEEP IT COMPLIMENTARY
Always compliment your date's appearance and personality.

ASK OPEN ENDED QUESTIONS
These questions set the tone to feed off reaction for cooking up *The Chocolate Flirt!*

KEEP A SENSE OF HUMOR
Keep conversation light and entertaining.

PAINT A PICTURE OF SEX APPEAL

Paint a picture of sex appeal by slowing down the voice, Gazing directly into their eyes, and implying the amazing possibilities of a future.

STUDY YOUR DATE

Take notes mentally on their mannerisms, conversations, and listen closely as they speak . The more you learn about your date in a short time, the easier it will be for you to perfect *The Chocolate Flirt*!

MAKE THEM FEEL LIKE A GOD / GODDESS

Make them feel like a GOD/GODDESS! Listen closely when they speak, and feed off those conversation pieces with special responses and compliments.

USE RAW CHOCOLATE

There is something about RAW Chocolate in its most naked form that screams Desire, so whether you cook up a SEXY recipe with CHOCOLATE, buy it, or order a heavenly CHOCOLATE dessert, therefore using raw chocolate will only enhance *The Chocolate Flirt*.

CONCLUSION

A SEXY Congrats, because you are on your way to becoming a leading Prince or Princess in cooking up a Tasty *Chocolate Orgy*! The next *Chocolate* episode is going to take the role of *The Chocolate Flirt* one step further by teaching you how to add a bit of Spiciness to a menu of Love with *The Chocolate Sizzle*....

Inside the Fortress,
Her fairytale of
Romance paused to a
Hopeless tune of
Love.

Outside, His lips
locked as he crossed
A stone entrance.
You can see the
Fire in his ocean
Blue eyes, Rising against
The tide of heartache,
Blazing with "I love you".
His light mane rustled
In the wild, as he began
To build a Fortress of
loyalty, Passion, and
Pleasure.

Together, their fortress
Cemented together, solidifying
A wreath of eternal
Love.

21
21A

CHOCOLATE EPISODE #3

The Chocolate Sizzle

Now that you've nailed the Spicy Flavor in cooking up *The Chocolate Flirt*, this Episode is going to *Sizzle* the *Spice* even farther!

The menu for creating one mouthwatering *Chocolate Orgy* lies in the recipe for *The Chocolate Sizzle*! Indeed it's true the recipe to creating an extraordinary Love lies in how well you *Sizzle* with Aphrodisiacs when it comes to *Cooking up Bittersweet Endings!*

Aphrodisiacs are the shaker and maker to one unforgettable night of Chocolate heaven. Indeed the same thing applies to the Category of Sizzling, where boiling to the right temperature of Passion allows you to cook with the Hottest Aphrodisiacs!

Whether you are a *Sizzler*, or are just a natural Fizzler, the Heat created in this *Episode* depends on your imagination. The last episode should have ignited the sparks of imagination as you took notes on becoming a *Chocolate Flirt*! On the other hand, if you ate up the information in the last chapter, your appetite should be primed for cooking up *The Chocolate Sizzle*! The next scene in this guide will have the top aphrodisiacs for a rock star *Chocolate Orgy!*

TOP 10 SEXY APHRODISIACS

1. **POMEGRANATES**
Drink this forbidden cocktail

2. **COCONUT WHIP CREAM**
Spoon feed a creamy mouthful

3. **CHOCOLATE FONDUE**
Dip raw pleasures in chocolate fondue

4. **CHILIS**
Spice up starters

5. **VANILLA**
Flavor with vanilla

6. **STRAWBERRIES**
Leave sensual notes with strawberries

7. **HONEY**
Drizzle love with honey

8. **AVOCADO**
Sizzle the temperature with avocado oil

9. **COFFEE**
Perk up desire in a chocolate latte

10. **WATERMELON**
Grind down to a watermelon smoothie

CONCLUSION

The world of Aphrodisiacs has seasoned the salt and pepper entrees in the world of Dating to a spicier Love Feast when it comes to Cooking up Bittersweet Endings! If you mastered the *Sizzle* over *Fizzle* when it comes to heating up Passion, then read on, because the next Chocolate Episode is all about dipping into the darker side of Fantasy with The Chocolate Seduction …

She galloped away
In the direction of
The burning candle,
Her mane wildly blew with
The fiery passion.

Into the moonlight
Her eyes sparkled
A story of
Fantasy, blazing romance to
The Dark stallion.

His eyes mesmerized
For her Arrival.
You can see the sweat
In his brow,
The story lines in his hands,
The blood in his heart, and
Unfinished good-byes that faded
Into long lost
Kisses.

Galloping together, they
Became one.

21
21A

CHOCOLATE EPISODE #4

The Chocolate Seduction

The Steamy Romance cooked up in the former episode of "The Chocolate Sizzle" has brought Passion back to those Vanilla Nights! This Episode is all about leaving behind burnt desserts in turn for a new melting point of Love, one where under Raw Desserts become a Magnet for The Chocolate Seduction!

The *Orgasmic* flavor Cooked up in *The Chocolate Seduction* boils down to how many ingredients of Raw Pleasure you dive into! Raw pleasure is the main ingredient in *The Chocolate Seduction*. In this *Chocolate Episode,* discover the Top Raw pleasures to cooking up *The Chocolate Seduction!*

TOP RAW PLEASURES TO COOKING
The Chocolate Seduction

SIZZLE WITH RAW OILS

Sizzling with oil from the start will turn up the heat for Passion when cooking up *The Chocolate Seduction*! (Focus on plant-based oils.)

ENHANCE DESIRE WITH RAW SWEETNESS

The recipe of *Desire* will get sweeter in Cooking up a *Chocolate Seduction* when you focus on the Raw Flavor of Sweets! The Raw Flavor of Sweets comes down to The Garden of Love where dipping into fruits of *Desire* become *Orgasmic*! These fruits of *Desire* are dates, bananas, figs, apples, strawberries, and peaches!

GET DOWN WITH RAW LOVE

Get down only with *Raw Love*, where no fake ingredients come between the *Bittersweet Ending* to Cooking up *The Chocolate Seduction*!

SPICE IT UP WITH RAW PASSION

Keep the flavor full of Raw Passion! Spice it up with cinnamon, nutmeg, chili, cardamom, cloves, ginger, saffron or pumpkin spice!

FINISH WITH A RAW MOUTHFUL

The Chocolate Seduction always ends on a *Naughty* note when you come with a Raw mouthful! The only way to melt a frozen Love is with just a mouthful of Chocolate Strawberries, edible flowers, Watermelon, Avocados, Pomegranate seeds, vanilla, honey, bananas, dates, basil, etc.

CONCLUSION

The steamy *Sizzle* that heated *The Chocolate Seduction* has ignited the Song "Love Struck" when it comes to falling for *Chocolate Love*! The wet aftertaste of *Chocolate* temptation from this *Redhot Episode* has found its way aboard an Erotic adventure, leaving the flavor of Vanilla at home, and thrusting towards a more Exotic destination, one where the forecast of Steamy Love becomes *hotter* for a new melting point of Lust, *The Chocolate Meltdown* …

The taste of chocolate
Melted their
Love affair into a
Heated romance.
You can tell
from her warm
touch, she was
The engine to igniting
His dreams.

As midnight struck,
The smell of vanilla,
the sight of flesh, and
The mark of red lipstick,
Fueled a race, where
Beautiful Destinations
Became Markers to
The Finish line.

The race brought them
Together as one, ranking
Number One for the
Victory of Love.

lights...

CAMERA...

ACTION!

CHOCOLATE EPISODE #5

The Chocolate Meltdown

The pure Raw taste of Desire whipped up in "The Chocolate Seduction" has increased the temperature of dessert time to a burning Desire for The Chocolate Meltdown!

This Chocolate Episode removes the bland aftertaste left behind from dry starters, flavorless Love feasts, and fake food-gasms! *The Chocolate Meltdown* will portray dessert as a way to get Hands On when it comes to getting down with the fruits of *Desire* and dipping into the darker flavor of Fantasy. The Bittersweet Ending cooking up in this Chocolate Episode is the most Erotic flavor in *The Chocolate Meltdown* yet!

COOKING TIPS FOR
The Chocolate Meltdown

WHIP UP SEDUCTION

When you are Cooking up a Fantasy, the sensory experience for *The Chocolate Meltdown* comes down to how you *Whip Up Seduction*. Are you one that speaks the language of "Babe" with phrases like "Baby, I want you," "Babe, you're driving me crazy," or "Baby, you are my heart"—or are you one that silently speaks with gestures over words by touching hands, massaging shoulders, or stroking hair? Whether you *Whip Up Seduction* with your verbal cues or body language, one thing that's for sure is the way in which you *Whip Up Seduction* will always determine how *hot* it gets!

INCREASE THE HEAT

The breathtaking Fantasy of *The Chocolate Meltdown* starts the moment you boil up the warmest temperature of *Lust*! Whether it's dancing salsa, or cooking up a Dessert Fetish, you need to step out of hard to *Swallow* starters, and focus on the ultra smooth taste of Wet starters! This starts the moment liquid fun enters the most erogenous zone, the mouth! Some favorites that increase blood flow the minute you Swallow are Red Wine, Ginseng tea, Hot Cocoa, Apple Martini, Coffee, Almond Smoothie, Watermelon infused drink, Coconut Water, Pomegranate Sangria!

GET INTO SKINNY DIPPING

Less is more when it comes to really cooking up a Sweaty Love for *The Chocolate Meltdown!* The act of Skinny Dipping down to a Raw Goodness when it comes to food and your Spirit will make *The Chocolate Meltdown* go down smoother and ignite fireworks of Passion for an *Orgasmic Chocolate Orgy!*

CONCLUSION

By now you should have tasted the richer flavor of Fantasy in *The Chocolate Meltdown*, leaving room only for a mouthful of Love, awaiting you in *The Chocolate French Kiss…*

TOP 10 FRUITS FOR SKINNY DIPPING INTO FANTASY
1. CHERRIES
2. APPLES
3. MANGOES
4. WATERMELON
5. RASPBERRIES
6. STRAWBERRIES
7. PAPAYAS
8. BANANAS
9. PINEAPPLE
10. FIGS

The aroma of
Freshly brewed
Passion boiled in
Her body, warming
Up a cold love affair.
The scent of espresso,
Filled the cafe, as
Their eyes locked.
The light in His
Ocean blue eyes
Unlatched a romance.

You can see from
Inside the window,
A broken story of
"I Love you", however
Her cappuccino colored
Eyes, long golden coffee
Colored hair, and mocha
lipstick, washed away
The bitter taste
From cold beginnings,
Displaying a new
Window of love.

LE COMPTOIR DE MATHILDE
RME
BEREIDE
OLADE
CHOCOLATS CHAUDS
hot chocolate

21
21A

CHOCOLATE EPISODE #6

The Chocolate French Kiss

The flavor of *Desire* from *The Chocolate Meltdown* has dripped into a more decadent flavor of *Je t'aime* (I love you)! In this *Chocolate* episode, *The Chocolate French Kiss* heightens the Climax of *Je t'aime* (I love you) to forbidden tryst of wet fun!

This *Chocolate Episode* will crown you The GOD or GODDESS when it comes to Kissing like heaven! If you enjoyed dipping into the darker side of Fantasy with *The Chocolate Meltdown*, then wait until you feast your eyes and tongue on this wet teaser because the Tempting flavors of wet fun are going to soak *Desire* beyond your Wildest Fantasies!

In this Episode, all your senses reach a Love Climax: Your mouth finds the flavor of Desire in juicy beginnings, your nose in the seductive pheromones of Vanilla, and your eyes gazing into the Pupil of *Lust*, and your tongue in an Erogenous area, as you discover a mouthwatering escapade in *The Chocolate French Kiss…*

SEXY INGREDIENTS TO PERFECTING
The Chocolate French Kiss

JUICY LIPS

The lips for both men and women are the magnet of *Desire*. In order to create the strongest magnetic force between you and Your Honey, you need to make the lips Juicy! Therefore, the lips need to be prepped with love and care, so for males you should use a chap stick that moisturizes, and for women make sure you use a lip gloss that creates a wet, plump, and enticing look. To really seal the deal, add a clear vanilla, cinnamon, or chocolate flavor to have your lips taste delish!

FRESH LOVE

Bring a whiff of fresh Love to your breath. Stay away from foods or substances that will ruin the freshness of the kiss, like garlic, coffee, onions, cheese, or cigarettes. Try breath mints, breath sprays, or gum in the flavors of peppermint, wintergreen, cinnamon, and vanilla.

THE EYE OF SEDUCTION

After you nailed the perfect Lips, then during the conversation, speak Seduction with your eyes. Keep conversation to basics cues during engagement with one word answers and nodding sometimes instead of speaking. Let your date take the lead in conversation as you gaze into their eyes, staring into the Pupil of *Lust*. Before moving forward, make sure they are ready to receive *The Chocolate French Kiss*.

TEASE FOR THE CLIMAX

Rather than heading right to the home base with massaging your partner's tongue with your tongue, you must tease for the Climax! You can do this by gently bringing their face closer to yours, and staring them directly into their *Pupil of Lust,* but not kissing just yet. Then, move their lips towards yours and tilt your head to the side, while making sure your lips are locked.

SLOW RHYTHM WITH LIPS

The best *Chocolate French Kisses* start slow using light pressure with the lips, and just the right amount of tongue. Remember, real Passion is slow and just the right amount of touching to get an in-sync rhythm. Then you are ready to open your mouth a little wider to signal your date you are ready for *The Chocolate French Kiss.*

HELLO SMALL TONGUE

Close your eyes, and relax by breathing through your nose. Introduce the tongue halfway, thus making sure your partner is ready to reciprocate, because Rhythm, and just the right amount of tongue, is the difference between an *Orgasmic Chocolate French Kiss,* and one that is Flavorless. Gently slip your tongue a little into your date's mouth, using light pressure, ensuring both of your tongues touch and become in sync. It's important you focus on The Sensuality of the Kiss, and just the right amount of tongue, and pressure is crucial in this step. An important thing to keep in mind is how deep you go. *The Chocolate French Kiss* is more focused on in-sync rhythm, light to moderate pressure, and a playful yet passionate Tongue Kiss!

MASTER THE SMALL TONGUE

It's important you master the Small Tongue step and the rhythm before progressing to an Advanced Chocolate French Kisses.

SPICE IT UP

Once you have established a harmonious rhythm between you and your Honey, and have mastered the former step, you can then begin to Spice it up. This comes from switching the speed of kisses to providing new sensations to *The Chocolate French Kiss.* If you have been dating a while, try using your hands to explore each other's body, gently touching and caressing both basic and Erogenous areas, including hair, ears, hips, chest, back, neck etc.

PRACTICE MAKES PERFECT

To become an expert at anything you have to practice, so the more time you spend kissing your date or Honey, the more you will discover their likes and dislikes, and vice versa. If the first *Chocolate French Kiss* isn't exploding with Euphoria, then you need go back and master the early steps of *Slow Rhythm With Lips* and *Master the Small Tongue.* These steps will make it possible for your lips and tongue to taste euphoria!

CONCLUSION

If you haven't locked tongues and swallowed up the Naughty flavor of *Chocolate French Kiss* yet, then you need to rewind! On the other hand, if you are starting to perform as that leading God or Goddess, then congrats because you are ready to explore the darker side of Fantasy with *The Chocolate Lick Down* …

The Ocean moved
Their love beyond
The cliff.
You could see the
Rocky Waves rustled his
Light Hair towards her
Chocolate eyes.
You could feel the
Crash of euphoria from their
Tears of joy.

After they floated in
Unison among the Ocean blue,
You could taste the
Bittersweet taste on
Their kisses.

The melody of the
Ocean blue soaked their
Heart with a mouthwatering
Romance.

21
21A

CHOCOLATE EPISODE #7

The Chocolate Lick Down

The Chocolate Orgy's verdict is finally in after the trial of the mouthwatering *Chocolate French Kiss.* The verdict to *The Chocolate French Kiss* is Guilty of being one *Smooth Date* for Dessert! All those smooth talking ingredients that perfected the *Chocolate French Kiss* have sent a heat wave of Passion for *The Chocolate Lick Down!*

The Chocolate Lick Down is heating up the battle of a *Kinky* appetite! When it comes to areas of *Sizzling* in *The Chocolate Lick Down*, you must get hands on with *Whipping, Spicing, Boiling, Role Plating, and Tasting.* This *Chocolate Episode* is going to *Fizzle* out the residue from the stickiest encounters while teaching you how to get Naughty with your tongue, hands, and body in the most frisky of ways! Get ready to dip, lick, and suck the night away with the *Chocolate Lick Down…*

Read on to discover the techniques that make Cooking up The Chocolate Lick Down a fun filled Fantasy…

THE TECHNIQUES OF
The Chocolate Lick Down

WHIP FOR RAW PLEASURE

The ingredient of *Desire* sets the mood for Whipping up Raw Pleasure when it comes to cooking up *The Chocolate Orgy*! Whether you whip up Passion for Sensual Oils, or Exotic ingredients, you must always come together with *Desire*!

SPICE TO ENTICE

The shaker or maker to perfecting *The Chocolate Lick Down* is all in the Kama sutra of Spices! Whether you settle on nutmeg, cinnamon or pumpkin spice, it's all in the shake down of wet vs. dry! Do you shake down more spice with wet over dry in cooking up a *Chocolate Orgy*? If you answered yes to either one, then congrats you are one step away to perfecting *The Chocolate Lick Down!*

BOIL UP LUST

Lust heats up the Raw Pleasure to record breaking temperatures in *The Chocolate Orgy*! In essence, a *Chocolate Lick Down* will not satisfy without the ingredient of *Lust*. Start the temperature of *Lust* on medium heat and then slowly increase with methods of *Spice to Entice, Whip for Raw Pleasure*, and *Tease to Please*! Please note the *Tease to Please* technique is focusing on teasing with the Raw Sweetness of Honey, coconut sugar, and fruits of *Desire* including strawberries, figs, bananas, apples etc!

ROLE PLATING WITH RAW FUN

To reach the temperature of the *Orgasmic Sizzle* in T*he Chocolate Lick Down*, you must get Hands on with Role Plating! The way you get down with raw fun in cooking up *The Chocolate Lick Down* starts with the thunder of imagination, striking down encounter after another. The lightning bolt of Desire comes from Role Plating with Raw Fun in *The Chocolate Lick Down*. Whether you are the leading with Hands on Activities when it comes to dressing up a plateful of Raw Goodness, or you are one that prefers to let your Honey Dominate, while you sit back and pleasurably watch, there is no wrong answer, because both the role of the leading performer and Viewer can build up a Climatic Taste to the Swallow!

TASTE FOR THE HAPPY ENDING

Once the lightning bolt of Desire has come into Role Plating with *The Chocolate Lick Down*, you are ready for one Tasty Love Affair! The Tasty Love affair comes from Hands on Activity when it comes to feeding each other hand in hand! Watch how your Honey or Date licks, bites, and swallows as you get Hands on with *The Chocolate Lick Down*. The Taste For The Happy Ending comes down to how you master the former steps: Whip For Raw Pleasure, Spice to Entice, Boil Up Lust, & Role Plating with Raw Fun!

CONCLUSION

The aftertaste of Sweetness left behind from *The Chocolate Lick Down* has dripped into an Erotic Menu full of *Chocolate Orgasms*, where warm encounters of passion exchange wet *Chocolate French Kisses* between you and your Honey! The next episode does some kissing and telling for creating one explosive *Chocolate Orgasm....*

Her soldier of love
Came to her rescue amidst
A dark storm.
Her battle of passion
Fired up from his
Warm touch. You can see his
His rugged face portrayed
An unfiltered romance to
Their fortress,
Brightening the greyest
Areas of Faith in her
Contrasting picture.
His ocean blue eyes
Soothed her broken
Vessel, renewing her
Breaths of love to flow
Beyond any cloudy
Doubt, where their
landscape of evergreens
became their
Victory of "I Do's"

21
21A

CHOCOLATE EPISODE #8

The Chocolate Orgasm

Now that you understand the ingredients to perfecting *The Chocolate French Kiss*, and the techniques to *Sizzling The Chocolate Lick Down*, the sweetest explosion to cooking up *The Chocolate Orgy* is only one menu away!

The date night to cooking up Steamy Love is all about creating the menu of *The Chocolate Orgasm*! The menu should start with playful appetizers that lead into a mouthwatering bites, and end on a sweet swallow!

It's important that you explore the world of SEXY Foods before planning the menu of *The Chocolate Orgasm*. The first part of this Episode is going to highlight the top SEXY foods that both you and your date should explore together before cooking up the menu of *The Chocolate Orgasm*.

THE TOP 5 SEXY FOODS IN
The Chocolate Orgasm

OYSTER MANIA

If you are ready to play the role of God or Goddess in the SEXY world of Dating, then just follow 18th century bad boy Casanova who ate 50 raw oysters a day! Eating this love food with it's unique pheromone smell of sweet and salty along with it's silky texture, and dopamine producing properties make it for one *Hot* night beyond the board, The kitchen board! Oysters do plant the seeds of Temptation by allowing you to get hands on with your Honey or Date! Start slow, and gaze into each other eyes, and then take the lead with this food to feed your Honey's appetite bite after bite.

CHILI PEPPER LOVE

When it comes to hitting a home run in the ball park game of love, chili peppers score on the top. Their compounds aid in releasing endorphins that boost mood and provide an energy surge. The compounds in Chili Peppers heat the body from the inside out, creating a night where layers of clothing don't exist! Capsaicin, the compound that causes chili's to burn will make the tongue tingle for a Passionate kiss!

FIFTY TALES OF VANILLA

Dating not only stirs up Desire, but it also adds a mysterious flavor to one's appetite. Is it possible to get your appetite to come into tasting Fifty Tales of Vanilla? The answer smells like a warm sweet YES where today Fifty Tales of Vanilla are practically helping you begin a new chapter of Love. From candles, oils, creams, perfume, foods, ingredients, and Erotic décor, Vanilla is becoming a superhero in cooking up a bittersweet ending! Whether you begin your dating story with a Vanilla flame, or end the night with an incredible vanilla dessert, don't underestimate the sexual prowess of Vanilla!

THE CHAMPAGNE FAIRYTALE

Every Fairytale always comes into a Happy Ending when there are bubbly giggles. There is something about a *Champagne Fairytale*, that tells a story of Passion, seduction, and *Desire*, starting with a slow Fizz and then ending on a bubbly note . The Champagne Fairytale is a canvass that allows you to paint a story of Seduction with *Desirable* chapters that spark Erotic headlines. Your *Champagne Fairytale* should always highlight specific chapters around a Fantasy that teases your Honey or Date with liquid gold!

CHOCOLATE HEARTS

The saying, "Two hearts become one" is quite true when it comes to dipping into *Chocolate*! The *Chocolate* turn on is playful when it comes to increasing *Lust*. Whether you get Frisky with *Chocolate* Fondue, flirty with *Chocolate* strawberries, or seductive with a fine piece of *Chocolate*, the heated Passion for *Chocolate* Hearts will always come into a Happy Ending!

THE FUNDAMENTALS OF
The Chocolate Orgasm

PICK A SEXY SIGNATURE DISH

To cook up a Bittersweet Ending all comes down to how SEXY you want your signature flavor to be when it comes to executing The Menu of The Chocolate Orgasm! To really go above traditional recipes when it comes to dishing out standard flavors, the SEXY Signature dish will begin with the appetizer. Make sure to add a splash of Desire, so your Date or Honey feels the heat of temptation rising.

Are you one who is spicy and warm, or one that becomes cool and sweet? Those that favor the first option usually cook spicy appetizers like guacamole, queso, or chili pepper tapas, where as those that prefer the second would most likely step foot in Margaritaville, a ceviche kingdom, or in a garden of Forbidden fruit.

ADD LIQUID FUN

Whether you opt for *The Champagne Fairytale*, or dip into wet side of *Chocolate* with Fondue, the component of Liquid adds a element of *Lust*! The type of Liquid fun you have comes down to how big your appetite is for a huge *Climax*! The more playful you get with sweeter liquids like tropical sangria, *Chocolate* fondue, and fruit smoothies, the more likely you will be cooking up a sweet drama! On the other hand, when you explore the warmer, and spicier flavor of liquid fun like soups, teas, coffees, liquor flavored drinks, and purees, the more chances you will be cooking up a *Bittersweet Ending*!

CREATE A MENU OF EROTIC FLAVOR

It's important to make sure the whole menu to creating a *Chocolate Orgasm* has an all star menu of Erotic flavor. This means the menu should include Erotic food throughout the Date including a mouthwatering appetizer, a juicy entree, and a decadent dessert! Whether you start the night nibbling on *Chocolate* covered strawberries or feed each other oysters, pick one Erotic food for each dish as you cook up Pleasure in satisfying your Honey's appetite!

COOK UP A JUICY MIDDLE

After you messed around with exploring the bites and nibbles of a SEXY signature starter, it's time to dive into a juicy middle. This part of the menu sets the tone for the dessert finale! To create a juicy middle you need a dish that has one of these elements: a bold flavor, an exotic spice, a bright color, or smooth texture! Whether you whip up a pasta primavera in red marinara sauce finished with mango shavings, or a seared Salmon in a coconut ginger sauce on a bed of black rice finished with wasabi, remember to keep the focus on creating a menu of Erotic Flavor, because that type of Flavor enhances the *Climax* of *The Chocolate Orgasm*!

ROLE PLAYING WITH DESSERT

After you nibbled the sexy starter, and *Swallowed* a juicy middle, "*The Best is yet to Come*" when it comes to cooking up an Explosive *Chocolate Orgasm*! The last part of *The Chocolate Orgasm* has to do with how Naughty your appetite is for Fetish and Fantasy within the category of *Role Playing With Dessert*. The bigger your appetite, the more pleasurable your experience in *Role Playing With Dessert* will be!

To really make *Role Playing With Dessert* arousing when it comes to Sizzling the night away, you must be spontaneous, Open, and Nakedly real! Whether you decide to get frisky with the Dessert Fetish, whip up a recipe for Fantasy, or add a *Kinky* flavor, you can't go wrong with *Role Playing with Dessert*!

CONCLUSION

The rich aftertaste from the leisure activities of *The Chocolate Orgasm* should have increased hunger for a fresh *Chocolate Episode*, one where steamy encounters, liquid fun, and Fetishy flavors contribute to an unforgettable Climax for one mouthwatering *Chocolate Orgy!* The next *Chocolate Episode* will elevate your *Chocolate Orgasm* to a Forbidden Fantasy, where anything goes in *The Hot Chocolate Affair* …

The Chocolate Fairytale

The scent of vanilla
Brought him
Closer to her
Touch.
The taste of hot
Chocolate melted
Cold "I love you's".

You could tell from
The stubble in his face,
The sparkle in his eyes,
The strong veins in his arms,
Bloody love began to pump
Harder, strengthening
Broken Arteries.

The after taste of the
Chocolate Rendezvous,
left their hands
knotted and their mouths
locked in a
Chocolate Fairytale.

21
21A

CHOCOLATE EPISODE #9

The HOT Chocolate Affair

All the flavors cooked up in the former *Chocolate Episodes* should have Stroked the deepest areas of Date night! If not then go back and taste each *Chocolate Episode* again! On the other hand, if your mouth is watering from the unique flavor in the past *Episode*, then congratulations because you are ready to finally say *bon appétit* to this guide!

This *Chocolate Episode* will put your tongue on all those *Chocolate flavors* from the past *Episodes when* it comes to cooking up the ideal *Chocolate Orgy! The HOT Chocolate Affair* is all about *Flirting with different flavors, Mixing in Wet fun, Spicing it up,* and *Sizzling in the Steam…*

THE RECIPE FOR A
HOT Chocolate Affair

FLIRT AROUND WITH DIFFERENT FLAVORS

Are you one who likes to skinny dip in the lighter yet sweeter side of *Chocolate,* or are you one that gets caught up in the darker side of drama? In order to truly know if you fall in the first or last category, you must be down to *Flirting Around with Different Flavors.* The act of flirting with more than one Flavor will make cooking up a *HOT Chocolate Affair* appetizing as you immerse into the bolder flavor of *Chocolate!*

MIX IN WET FUN

Do you prefer the smooth and rich taste of *Chocolate* Milk over the mildly sweet tasting Almond Smoothie? Whether you decide to *swallow* the Milk or drink up the Smoothie, the element of mixing in wet ingredients never fails in cooking up the ideal recipe for *The HOT Chocolate Affair.* To perfect the recipe of *The HOT Chocolate Affair,* you need to turn up the temperature of Passion up as you *Mix in Wet Fun!*

SPICE IT UP

Surprise, Surprise … the secret is out when it comes to spicing up *The HOT Chocolate Affair,* and it has to do with *Falling Head over Heels* for the Spice of Fetish! The question becomes how does one *Fall Head over Heels* in Love for Fetish? The answer lies in our inherent *Desire* for Something *Exotic* which leads to our curiosity to spice it up with Fetish! Indeed, Fetish is the core ingredient for bringing *The HOT Chocolate Affair* to a boiling point of *Lust!*

SIZZLE IN THE STEAM

The after party to tasting the spice of Fetish should be one that starts to Steam *Desire* . When the *Lust* starts to bubble, the Steamy Encounters begin to activate those pleasure neurons for a Happy Ending. To really *Sizzle* in a Steamy Encounter, make sure you and your honey are both on the same page when it comes to being hands on with Raw ingredients, and using the Spice of Fetish!

CONCLUSION

The orgasmic *swallow* of this *Episode* should have you feeling like *Superman* or *Superwoman*! If your not quite there yet, then go back to the beginning of *The HOT Chocolate Affair*, so those ingredients can Cook up your *Desires* to a Euphoric Recipe. On the other hand, if your *Sizzling* with a Steamy *Desire*, then you are ready to bite into the finale of *The Chocolate Orgy,* where a Heavenly Fantasy awaits you in *The Bittersweet Ending . . . .*

The taste of the
Chocolate Cappuccino
Began to increase her
Thirst for a
Mouthwatering night.
She began to cook
Flavor that Sizzled
A dreamy romance.
You can see in the
The Dreamy romance,
A love affair
beginning to boil
A steamy picture, where
Chocolate Kisses, red roses,
And A Hot Chocolate Affair
Brought the two together for
Breathless moments, one
after another…

THE
FOOD ORGY
MICHELLE LYNN

21
21A

CHOCOLATE EPISODE #10

The Bittersweet Ending

Now that you understand how to Steam up *The HOT Chocolate Affair,* you can really perfect *The Bittersweet Ending*! This guide is intended for you to cook up a *Sizzling,* Steamy, and Spicy Date night, so the richer flavor of Love is always one mouthful away!

By now the wet fun from The HOT Chocolate Affair should have melted cold starters, leaving a hunger for the taste of Erotica. When it comes to truly scoring Flavor, taste, and satisfaction in this guide, you must end the final course with a Bittersweet Ending.

The final menu should read, smell, and look like a Fantasy! From delectable appetizers to playful entrees to tantalizing drinks, *The Bittersweet Ending* reflects the sweetest Fantasy where a dessert table reflects a fairytale of Sensuality, Passion, and Flavor. Here are the top tips to creating a dessert Fantasy that displays *The Bittersweet Ending…*

TIPS TO CREATING A
Dessert Fantasy

CREATE A THEME OF SENSUALITY

The taste of *The Bittersweet Ending* comes down to how well you Cook up Sensuality. Does your Dessert Fantasy use the richer ingredients of Passion focusing only on *The Bittersweet Ending* or do you prefer the sweeter ingredients of Fantasy focusing on slices of vanilla, berry good kisses and *Chocolate* waterfalls? Remember to make sure your theme of Sensuality has personal touches with notes, pictures, or past experiences that you both had shared in capturing Raw Love!

ELEVATE THE HEIGHT OF TEMPTATION

The height of temptation is the icing on the cake to a dessert Fantasy. Therefore it's essential your dessert Fantasy elevates temptation in *The Bittersweet Ending*. Therefore, you can use many different things to elevate the height of temptation in your dessert Fantasy like a *Chocolate* Waterfall (fondue fountain), an assortment of desserts, and a plateful of luscious strawberries. You can also add a dimension of temptation with roses, and whimsical objects that create a heavenly fantasy.

MAGNETIZE DESIRE WITH BITE SIZE LOVE

Desire speaks to us on so many levels thorough sight, smell, and taste. You can really magnetize *Desire* in your dessert fantasy by having a variety of bite size Love desserts. This automatically enhances the desire to become playful with each other by feeding each other bite size love!

SPARKLE WITH PASSION

To really make your dessert Fantasy shine into the nightfall, you need to sparkle Passion. Whether it's leaving personalized notes or memorabilia around the dessert Fantasy, or catering the menu of Sensuality to a specific *Desire*. The Passion always will sparkle when it comes to creating the design around your Date's *Desires*. Remember, the shades of darker designs play up a forbidden Fantasy, where as light colors of silver and white play up a fairytale Fantasy.

ROLE PLAY DESSERT INTO A FAIRYTALE

By now your Dessert Fantasy should smell, taste, and feel like Heaven. The fresh scent of Vanilla, and the melted *Chocolate* berry kisses should have touched the most Erogenous spots, igniting the sparks of spontaneity into a fiery drama of role playing that magically transforms a dessert Fantasy into a Fairytale. Finally, after the role playing has ended, your ability to step out of character and into the Moment becomes Candid as your *Desires* from you heart come true in the fairytale of Love!

CONCLUSION

The *Orgasmic Bittersweet Ending* of this *episode* should have you screaming "I do" to *The Chocolate Orgy*! However, If you are still whispering versus screaming YES!, then it's time to change your Recipe of Love, and repeat.

Get ready now to say *bon appétit* to a New "I Love You" when it comes to cooking up a Rich flavor of Love in your *Chocolate Orgy*! The second part of this Dating Guide has recipes that are fresh in flavor and are going to make your *Chocolate Orgy* surpass your wildest Fantasies, so get ready to grab some, *Chocolate*, oysters, strawberries and a SEXY Apron…

Their encounter left
Them hungry for
A one of a kind
love.

You can tell from
His ocean blue eyes,
His strong hands, and
Rugged looks, his
Appetite had changed.
Her pink lips, wild
Caramel hair, and
Almond shape eyes
Became the story
Flame burning in
His eyes.

The portrait of
Their romance was
Finely touched with
A rosy glow of passion.
The smell of pink
Roses welcomed
A new love
Affair.

THE FANTASY RECIPES FOR
The Chocolate Orgy

GF- GLUTEN FREE | DF- DAIRY FREE | V- VEGAN | VEG- VEGETARIAN

THE LOVE MAGNET

SERVES Temptation and a Sweet Flavor of Love
TIME 10 minutes

INGREDIENTS

1 tray	circular clear food tray
bundle	napkins, love inspired design or neutral colors (use enough to cover the tray)
15-20	cookies, light colored
15-25	chocolate candies, same size
1-4	strawberries

DIRECTIONS

1. Take a clear tray in a circular shape and cover it with the napkins
2. Create a design with the light cookies and treats by making a contrasting pattern with the chocolate candies in a clockwise direction. See Picture examples.
3. Look at the design and fill in gaps with the design to blend. This is the part where you become creative in shaping your design.
4. Place the desired amount of strawberries in the center of your design, or scattered around the design. This step will speak volumes of your Excitement towards your date!

This recipe pairs with every fantasy
recipe in *The Chocolate Orgy*

THE FLIRTY STARTERS

SERVES   Teasing starters and mouthwatering moments
TIME   20 minutes

MAKE VEGAN / GLUTEN FREE Buy Gluten free crackers, and replace the turkey with marinated tofu.

INGREDIENTS

1	box crackers, assorted, optional gluten free
1 cup	olives, Marinated Trio from Trader Joes
1 cup	turkey deli meat, Smoked from Applegate
½ cup	cucumber, rounds, sliced
½ cup	hummus
½ cup	salsa
2 tbsp	almond butter
1	lemon, slices, quartered
¼ cup	blueberries

DIRECTIONS

1. Cover a clear circular tray, with romantic themed napkins.
2. Next, use crackers from an assortment. Scatter the different types of crackers, using the same amount of each. For example, if your total is 16, you would be using 4 of each type of cracker.
3. Create 4 different kinds of cracker, as followed above: Make one cracker with cucumber rounds and olives, and another cracker have almond butter with blueberries, and another cracker have smoked turkey pieces with a tiny amount of salsa, and the last cracker have hummus with a lemon slice. (see picture)
4. Repeat this cracker recipe set up a few times and then begin to take some extra food and design the flirty starters. To make the tray pop, spread extra olives in the center, crackers and salsa at the ends, and at the opposite end add the hummus.
5. Finally, make sure *The Flirty Starters* looks appealing to the eye before serving to your Honey!

> This recipe goes well with every
> recipe in this section

THE SEX POT OYSTERS

SERVES   2
TIME   40 MINUTES   (DF, GF)

INGREDIENTS

8	oysters, opened (the seafood department will do this)
1 ½ cups	veggie Broth
2 ½ tbsp	olive oil
¼ cup	white onions, diced
¼ cup	basil, chopped
3 cloves	garlic, minced
1 cup	pureed tomatoes
1 tbsp	lemon herb seasoning
1 tsp	thyme
½ tsp	sea salt
½ tsp	pepper
1 tsp	stevia
1	lemon, squeezed

Garnish: Chopped greens, and lemons

DIRECTIONS

1. Preheat the oven to 400 degrees Fahrenheit.
2. Next, take a shallow roasting pan and add veggie broth.
3. Add olive oil and mix around before adding tomato puree, onions and seasoning.
4. Squeeze lemon juice and then add stevia. Mix around.
5. Spread oysters evenly above the mixture. Put in the oven for 20 minutes, before taking out and then using a spoon to put the mixture over the oysters, and then put oysters back in the oven for around 20- 25 minutes at a reduced temperature of 375 degrees Fahrenheit.
6. Take out and serve on a bed of chopped greens that have olive oil, and lemon juice.

> To really make your honey's mouth water serve with any of these recommended recipes: *The Orange Berry Champagne Fairytale* or *The Flirty Starters*

THE SULTRY CHOCOLATE SOUP

SERVES	2	
TIME	20 MINUTES	(DF, GF, Veg)

INGREDIENTS

2 cups	coconut milk, unsweetened
1 cup	hazelnut almond coconut creamer, *Califa farm*
2 tbsp	coconut nectar
1 tbsp	cacao
1 tsp	cinnamon
3 tbsp	chocolate chips, vegan
2	chocolate squares, *Go Raw Chocolate*
2 tbsp	cornstarch
3 tbsp	water

ALMOND COCONUT MARSHMALLOW TOPPING

1 tbsp	grape seed oil
¼ cup	almond Ricotta Cheese, *Kite hill* brand
3	marshmallows, gluten free, (broken into pieces)
2 tbsp	coconut nectar
1 tsp	cinnamon

Garnish:	Marshmallows, fresh mint, strawberries, and chocolate chips

DIRECTIONS

1. In a boiling pan, heat oil to medium. Add coconut milk, coconut creamer, cinnamon and 1 tbsp of cacao. Mix around the pot stirring cacao powder evenly.
2. Add chocolate chips and 2 Go Raw chocolate squares. As the chocolate melts, in a small bowl mix the corn starch with 3 tbsp of water until it's completely mixed. Then add the corn starch to the chocolate soup in the boiling pot.
3. Make sure soup comes to a boil and then reduce to a lower heat, and at. You want to have the soup thicken slightly in consistency before turning off the heat.
4. For the marshmallow topping, add one tablespoon of oil in a smaller boiling pot. Add 1/3 Cup of Kite Hill Almond ricotta cheese, and break up the marshmallows as you add them in the pot. Add two tablespoons of coconut nectar, and then mix really well so the marshmallows and the ricotta cheese begin to blend together. Add cinnamon and continue to cook until the marshmallows and cheese blend together evenly.
5. Then get a small soup bowl and pour the first serving of soup. Add the marshmallow topping on the side, and garnish with strawberries, fresh mint, and chocolate chips

To really make your honey's mouth water,
serve with any of these recommended recipes:
*The Tray of Flirty Starters, Lemon Pie Pumpkin
Bliss, A Chocolate Banana Cake Fantasy*

TURN ME ON KALE FIG SALAD IN A KEY LIME AVOCADO DRESSING

SERVES   2
TIME   15 MINUTES   (DF, GF, V)

INGREDIENTS

2 ½ cups	kale, chopped, divide into 2 plates
¼ cup	blueberries, divide into 2
¼ cup	carrots, shreds, divide into two
¼ cup	mozzarella, vegan *Miyoko's* brand, in small pieces, divided into 2
6	figs, halved, divided into 2

DRESSING

1 avocado, peeled pitted

⅔ cup macadamia milk, vanilla

1 ½ limes, squeezed

1 ½ tsp Stevia

1 tbsp apple cider vinegar

3 tbspgrape seed oil

¼ tsp sea salt

2 tbsp cilantro

DIRECTIONS

1. Divide the washed and chopped greens into two separate plates.
2. Divide the blueberries, carrot shreds, vegan cheese and halved figs evenly amongst the two plates.
3. For dressing use a blender to blend the ingredients and dress the salad lightly.

> To really make your honey's mouth water serve with any of these recommended recipes: *The Tray of Flirty Starters* and *The Orange Berry Champagne Fairytale*

THE PLAYFUL PIZZA ROUNDS

SERVES 3
TIME 20 MINUTES (DF, GF, Veg)

INGREDIENTS

1	pizza rounds, *Rustic Crust Old World Pizza* (GF)
1 cup	tomato sauce, organic with garlic and basil
2 tbsp	olive oil
¼ tsp	sea salt
¼ tsp	white pepper
1 tsp	oregano
2 tbsp	spinach, diced
¼ cup	cherry tomato, halves
4 tbsp	mozzarella cheese, vegan recommended

DIRECTIONS

1. Preheat the oven to 400 degrees. Coat baking sheet with olive oil.
2. Next spread the two gluten free crust on the pan and coat with olive oil and tomato sauce.
3. Season lightly with salt, pepper, and oregano.
4. Spread the cherry tomato halves evenly on each pizza. Then sprinkle the diced spinach and your choice of shredded mozzarella cheese, either dairy or dairy free.
5. Put pizza rounds in the oven for around 13- 15 minutes. Make sure you see pizza crust turning brown and crispy before taking out.
6. Let pizza rounds cool before you delightfully feed each!

To really make your honey's mouth water
serve with any of these recommended recipes:
The Orange Berry Champagne Fairytale and
The Pick me up Blueberry Smoothie

THE PICK ME UP
BLUEBERRY SMOOTHIE

SERVES   2
TIME   5 MINUTES   (DF, GF, V)

INGREDIENTS

15 oz	blueberries, frozen
11 oz	vanilla Protein drink, Orgain (1 shake)
2	dates
1 tsp	cinnamon
3 tsp	cilantro, chopped

Garnish: **Cilantro, blueberries, dark chocolate**

DIRECTIONS

1. Blend all the ingredients above and serve in one large mason jar or divide into two wine cups. Then Garnish with excitement for blueberries and dark chocolate!

> To really make your honey's mouth water serve with any of these recommended recipes: *The Tray of Flirty Starters, The Love Magnet, The Orgasmic Chocolate Covered Strawberries*

A DREAMY CHOCOLATE PEPPERMINT SMOOTHIE

SERVES 2
TIME 5 MINUTES (DF, GF, V)

INGREDIENTS

1	banana
8 oz	bananas, frozen *Woodstock* brand
2 cups	chocolate peppermint almond milk (*Trader Joe's* brand or you can replace by mixing 1 tbsp of cocoa, 1 tbsp of stevia, 2 Cups of vanilla almond milk, 1 tbsp of peppermint extract)
¼ cup	coconut whip cream, *So Delish* Brand
¼ cup	mint, chopped
2 tbsp	chocolate chips (Vegan, *Dream Brand*)
6 oz	coconut yogurt

Garnish: **Starlight mints, whip cream (dairy or dairy free), or fresh mint**

DIRECTIONS

1. Blend all the ingredients with love and serve in one large mason jar or divide into two wine cups. Then garnish with love!

> To really make your honey's mouth water
> serve with any of these recommended recipes:
> *The Lemon Pumpkin Pie Bliss, The Sweetest
> Date Cake, The Naughty Chocolate Cake*

QUALITY
EST 1926

THE ORANGE BERRY CHAMPAGNE FAIRYTALE

SERVES	16
TIME	5 MINUTES (DF, GF, V)

INGREDIENTS

24.5 oz	raspberry cranberry spritzer (1 bottle)
25 oz	sparkling white wine or champagne (1 bottle)
1	orange, squeezed
1	orange, quartered
½ cup	raspberries, halved

Garnish: **Orange slices, raspberries, chocolate squares**

DIRECTIONS

1. In a large clear vase or glass drink dispenser, add the sparkling cranberry raspberry spritzer, and then the Champagne or sparkling white wine. Mix both before squeezing the juice from the orange into the mixture. Then mix again before adding the chopped fruit.
2. Add the quartered oranges and the raspberry halves into the liquid.
3. Before serving, make sure your Champagne Fairytale is chilled in the fridge for 30 minutes .
4. Garnish with sweet treats!
5. Serve passionately in one large mason jar or divide into two wine cups to drink the night away!

> To really make your honey's mouth water serve with any of these recommended recipes: *The Sex Pot Oysters, The Flirty Starters, The Love Magnet*

A MOUTHWATERING MANGO SMOOTHIE

SERVES   2
TIME   5 MINUTES   (DF, GF, V)

INGREDIENTS

2 ¼ cups	mangoes, frozen
2/3 cup	pumpkin puree
2	dates, remove pits
1 cup	coconut milk, vanilla unsweetened
½ cup	raspberries, halved
2 tbsp	cashew Butter
½ tbsp	cinnamon
1 tsp	pumpkin Spice

Garnish: **Coconut whip cream, vegan chocolate chips, granola (GF), and coconut flakes**

DIRECTIONS

1. Blend all the ingredients with love and serve in two small dish cups. Then Garnish with Passion!

To really make your honey's mouth water serve with any of these recommended recipes: *The Naughty Chocolate Cake, The Cookie Fetish, The Sultry Chocolate Soup, The Beloved Brownies*

A CHOCOLATE BANANA SHAKE FANTASY

SERVES 2
TIME 10 MINUTES (DF, GF, V)

INGREDIENTS

8 oz bananas, frozen, *Woodstock* brand
5 oz macadamia nut milk, vanilla
1 ½ coconut date roll or dates
5 oz coconut yogurt, chocolate, *So Delish* Brand
1 tbsp vanilla Extract
½ tsp cinnamon
¼ cup vegan chocolate chips, *Dream* brand
1 tbsp grape seed oil (for melting chocolate chips)

Garnish: **Date roll slices, banana slices, and chocolate drizzle**

DIRECTIONS

1. Heat iron skillet to medium heat. Add grape seed oil and then add ¼ Cup of vegan chips. Let the chocolate melt completely.
2. As the chocolate is melting, add bananas, nut milk, coconut date rolls, chocolate coconut yogurt, cinnamon, and vanilla extract to a blender. Then blend until in liquid form.
3. Then once the chocolate has melted, add two tablespoons of melted chocolate to the blender and then mix.
4. Then serve with banana slices, chocolate chips, and chocolate drizzle.
5. Enjoy this Fantasy shake together!

> To really make your honey's mouth water serve with any of these recommended recipes: *The Orgasmic Chocolate Covered Strawberries, The Naughty Chocolate Cake, The Cookie Fetish*

THE HOT CHOCOLATE AFFAIR

SERVES 2
TIME 5 MINUTES (DF, GF, V)

INGREDIENTS

3½ cups	coconut milk
2 tbsp	cocoa, unsweetened
1 tbsp	coconut oil
3 tbsp	maple syrup
2 tbsp	chocolate chips, vegan
½ tsp	cinnamon

Garnish: **Coconut whip cream or dairy whip cream, strawberries, and chocolate chips**

DIRECTIONS

1. Heat sauté pan to medium heat. Add 3 Cups of coconut milk, cocoa, coconut oil and chips.
2. Mix around the cocoa and chips so the milk becomes smooth with the chocolate.
3. Increase heat to high temperature, so chips melt. As soon as the chips melt, add another ½ Cup of coconut milk and then add 3 tbsp of maple syrup. Reduce heat to a lower temperature.
4. Finally, add the spice of cinnamon once the chocolate has completely melted and the cocoa has mixed in.
5. Serve with a mouthful of coconut whip cream and decorate with Love in serving up mouthwatering strawberries and whip cream!

To really make your honey's mouth water serve with any of these recommended recipes: *The Orgasmic Chocolate Covered Strawberries, The Naughty Chocolate Cake, The Happy Ending Date Cake*

FORBIDDEN CHOCOLATE FIG BROWNIES

SERVES 7

TIME 1 HOUR   (DF, GF, V)

INGREDIENTS
Brownie

1 can white beans
¾ cup oat flour
2 tbsp cashew butter
⅓ cup figs

½ cup coconut milk
½ cup honey
¼ tsp salt
1 cup blueberries

Blueberry Frosting

1 ½ Cups frozen blueberries
1 ½ bananas, small
2/3 Cup coconut milk

avocado, small
1 Tbsp stevia
4 leaves mint

Garnish: **Coconut whip cream, mint, blueberries, and vegan chocolate chips**

DIRECTIONS

1. Preheat the oven to 375 degrees Fahrenheit. Take a small square cake pan and coast with plant based oil.
2. In a blender add all liquid ingredients, except the oat flour and blueberries. Then, add the oat flour, and blend.
3. Transfer the batter to the pan and then place in the oven for 30 minutes.
4. Remove from oven and place in the freezer for 30 minutes.
5. For the blueberry frosting, add all the ingredients to a blender, and mix. Once finished, put in the freezer for just 15 minutes.
6. After the brownies have hardened, add coconut whip cream and blueberry frosting with fresh mint and dark Chocolate.
7. Have fun feeding each other with this sweet treat!

> To really make your honey's mouth water serve with any of these recommended recipes: *The Love Magnet, The Flirty Starters, The Orange Berry Champagne Fairytale*

A NUTTY LOVE FOR BANANAS IN A BERRY PARFAIT

SERVES   3
TIME   35 MINUTES   (DF, GF, V)

INGREDIENTS

Parfait Crust

1 cup oats, gluten free
1½ bananas, small
½ cup apple sauce, unsweetened

2 tbsp cashew butter
⅓ cup cashew pieces
½ tsp cinnamon

Berry Puree

10 oz frozen berries
1 cup almond vanilla yogurt,
    Kitehill brand

¼ Cup coconut whip cream, *So
    Delish* Brand
1 tsp cinnamon

Garnish: **Granola, almond vanilla yogurt, vegan chocolate chips**

DIRECTIONS

1. In a blender add all the parfait crust ingredients and blend. Then take out either two mini mason jars, an ice cream serving dish, or a large mason jar. Transfer the crust to bottom half of dish or dishes, leaving enough room for the berry mixture, and whip cream or yogurt topping.
2. Then put the glass dish in the freezer 30 minutes.
3. In a clean blender, add all the ingredients for the berry puree mix and blend. Then put in the freezer for 15 minutes before pouring on the Oat Banana Crust.
4. Top with vanilla yogurt, coconut whip cream, and garnish with Raw Passion!

To really make your honey's mouth water serve with any of these recommended recipes: *The Love Magnet, The Flirty Starters, The Orange Berry Champagne Fairytale, The Mouthwatering Mango Smoothie*

THE LEMON PUMPKIN PIE BLISS

SERVES 9
TIME 90 MINUTES   (DF, GF, Veg)

INGREDIENTS

Crust

1 cup oats
1½ cups granola, sprouted
   cinnamon One Degree
   Organics
10 dates, (Soak in water for
   five minutes, remove pits)

1 cup cashew pieces
lemon, Squeezed
1 tbsp lemon extract
1 tbsp grape seed oil
1 tbsp pumpkin spice

Filling

2 eggs
16 oz pumpkin puree
1 cup coconut milk
1 tbsp grape seed oil
½ tsp sea salt
½ tbsp cinnamon

½ tbsp pumpkin spice
3 tbsp maple Syrup
⅔ cup stevia
1 lemon, squeezed
1 tbsp lemon extract

Garnish: **Vanilla coconut ice cream, cinnamon, baked
pears or apples**

DIRECTIONS

1. Preheat oven to 425 degrees.
2. Make sure you soak all dates in a cup water for a few minutes before adding to blender, so they are easy to blend.
3. In a blender, add all the crust ingredients and pulse.
4. Transfer raw crust from blender to pie pan and start forming crust around the pie pan. Then set aside.
5. In a large bowl, crack the eggs and beat vuntil even.
6. Add all pumpkin puree, coconut milk, and maple syrup and mix until even.
7. Add stevia, pumpkin pie spice, cinnamon and mix.
8. Once all ingredients for the filling have mixed, add the lemon extract and squeezed lemon. Make sure you really mix the lemon juice.
9. Transfer pumpkin batter to crust and spread evenly.
10. Next, put the pie in for 15 minutes at 425 degrees, and then reduce heat to 350 degrees for the next 40 minutes.
11. Take out after a total time of 55-60 minutes and let pie cool.
12. Serve with your favorite flavor of ice cream, either dairy or dairy free, and your choice of baked fruit.
13. Finally, enjoy feeding each bliss as you gaze deeply into each other eyes!

To really make your honey's mouth water serve with any of these recommended recipes: This recipe goes well with *The Love Magnet, The Flirty Starters, A Dreamy Peppermint Smoothie*

THE HAPPY ENDING DATE CAKE

SERVES 9
TIME 75 MINUTES (DF, GF, Veg)

INGREDIENTS

Cake

1½ cup buckwheat flour
½ cup coconut flour
4 eggs
½ lemon, juice squeezed
2 cup coconut milk, vanilla
½ cup stevia
8 oz apple sauce, unsweetened

4 tbsp honey
¼ tsp salt
1 ½ tbsp baking soda
12 dates (soak in water)
½ cup coconut water
1 tbsp coconut Oil – for bundt
  cake pan

Frosting Puree

1 cup strawberries, frozen   ½ cup coconut water
1 banana   1 tbsp maple syrup

Garnish: **Chocolate coconut ice cream, strawberries, and vegan chocolate chips**

DIRECTIONS

1. Preheat the oven to 375 degrees.
2. Add eggs and beat until mixed. Then add lemon juice and mix. Add all liquid ingredients except coconut water, and add soaked dates. Make sure you soak dates for at least five to ten minutes in a cup full of water. Mix the ingredients before adding dry ingredients of coconut flour, buckwheat flour, salt, stevia, and baking soda. Add coconut water last.
3. Take out a baking bundt pan and coat with 1 tbsp of plant based oil. Transfer batter to bundt pan and spread evenly around pan. Then put in the oven for 40-45 minutes. Check around 40 minutes to make sure cake is golden brown and you can test with a pick to see if the batter is cooked. If the pick comes out clean with no dough or batter, then it's ready to be taken out. If not leave in for five more minutes.
4. Let the cake cool for 15 minutes before serving with frosting puree. Blend all ingredients in the blender for the frosting puree, and then garnish with chocolate coconut ice cream, strawberries, and vegan chocolate chips.

> To really make your honey's mouth water serve with any of these recommended recipes: *The Love Magnet, The Flirty Starters, The Orange Berry Champagne Fairytale*

LIP SMACKING MAPLE DATE
CHOCOLATE CHIP COOKIES

SERVES   14
TIME   40 MINUTES   (DF, GF, V)

INGREDIENTS

1 egg	¼ Cup stevia
1 Cup oat flour	1 tbsp baking powder
1/4 Cup grape seed oil	½ Cup oats, gluten free
½ Cup coconut Vanilla yogurt, or use Soy	2 tbsp chocolate chips, vegan, *Dream* Brand
1/3 Cup maple Syrup	2 tbsp dates, pieces, diced

Garnish: **Vegan chocolate chips, coconut whip cream, and vanilla coconut ice cream**

DIRECTIONS

1. Preheat oven to 350 degrees Fahrenheit. Then in medium bowl crack egg, and beat until the yolk is even.
2. Add yogurt, and rest of wet ingredients.
3. Add dry ingredients to the wet ingredients and mix.
4. Fold in chocolate chips and date pieces last.
5. Take a large cookie sheet, and then coat with plant based oil.
6. Then spoon cookie dough into small balls, and then space them out evenly apart on the tray. Repeat process until you are finished with the dough. Then leave in the oven for 15-20 minutes. Check around 15 minutes to see if cookies are golden, and if they are then take out and let the cookies cool for 15 minutes.
7. Serve with a mouthful of coconut whip cream or coconut vanilla ice cream.

To really make your honey's mouth water serve with any of these recommended recipes: *The Love Magnet, The Flirty Starters, The Orange Berry Champagne Fairytale, The Mouthwatering Mango Smoothie*

THE BELOVED BROWNIES

SERVES 10
TIME 75 MINUTES (DF, GF, V)

INGREDIENTS

5 oz	vanilla almond yogurt
15 oz	pumpkin puree (1 can)
1 cup	carob chips, melted, vegan (can use chocolate too)
4 tbsp	grape seed oil
3 tbsp	maple Syrup
½ cup	cacao
1 tsp	cinnamon

Garnish: **Strawberries, coconut flakes, and coconut vanilla ice cream**

DIRECTIONS

1. Heat iron skillet to medium. Add 1 tbsp of grape seed oil and wait until the sauté pan gets hot before adding carob chips. You can also use vegan or non vegan chocolate chips in replacement of carob chips.
2. As the chocolate melts, combine ingredients of pumpkin puree: 3 tbsp of grape seed oil, 5 oz vanilla almond yogurt, ½ cup cacao, 1 tsp of cinnamon, and 3 tbsp of maple syrup.
3. Mix until batter is even, and then scoop up the melted chocolate from the pan, and add to the bowl.
4. Mix again until the batter is smooth in form.
5. Transfer batter and spread evenly in a 9" baking pan.
6. Put in the freezer for 65 minutes until it's extra firm.
7. Garnish with strawberries and coconut vanilla ice cream.

> To really make your honey's mouth water
> serve with any of these recommended
> recipes: *The Love Magnet, The Flirty Starters,*
> *The Orange Berry Champagne Fairytale*

THE EUPHORIC BUTTERNUT SQUASH PIE

SERVES 7
TIME 90 MINUTES   (DF, GF, V)

INGREDIENTS

Crust

1½ cups	cashews, chopped
9	dates, soak in water and remove pits
2 ¼ cups	oats, gluten Free
1 cup	graham cracker pie crust, gluten free, vegan (use graham crackers crumbled)

Frosting

3 cups butternut squash, cubed, cooked
1 tbsp grape seed oil
¼ cup honey

2 tbsp apple sauce, unsweetened
2 tbsp cashew butter
1 tsp cinnamon

Garnish: **Dried cranberries, oats, coconut whip cream, dark chocolate**

DIRECTIONS

1. Cook butternut squash for five to eight minutes on a medium heat before adding to blender.
2. Soak dates in a cup of water for five minutes so they get soft enough to blend down into a crust.
3. In a blender add all ingredients for the crust and blend.
4. Then transfer crust from blender to a pie pan. Use your hands to form the shape of the crust around the pie pan. Please note any extra dough you can use in either a muffin tray or cookie sheet, forming a muffin or cookie shape.
5. Put the crust in the freezer for 30 minutes, so it can get firm.
6. Right before taking out the crust, blend all frosting ingredients in a blender. Then, take out pie crust and decorate with the frosting forming a medium circle in the center of the pie crust. (see picture).
7. Put in the freezer for another 45 minutes, and then top with dried fruits, oats, and coconut whip cream!

This goes great with The Love Magnet, The Flirty Starters, The Orange Berry Champagne Fairytale, The Mouthwatering Mango Smoothie, The Hot Chocolate Affair

THE COOKIE FETISH

SERVES   12
TIME   40 MINUTES   (DF, GF, V)

INGREDIENTS

10	dates, soak in water and remove pits
1	cup cashews, pieces, chopped
1	cup oats, gluten free
2 tbsp	cacao
2 tbsp	almond butter, Crunchy kind from *Trader Joes*
2 tbsp	chocolate chips, vegan

Garnish: **Strawberries, coconut vanilla ice cream, and vegan chocolate chips**

DIRECTIONS

1. Prepare a baking sheet with parchment paper.
2. Remove all pits from dates. Then soak all the dates together in a cup of water for around three to five minutes before adding to blender.
3. After dates are very soft, add them to blender along with cashews, oats, and cacao, and almond butter.
4. Then fold chocolate chips into batter.
5. Take a tablespoon of cookie batter and roll into a ball shape and then flatten into a cookie, and place on cookie sheet. Repeat this process until you have no more dough left.
6. Then put baking sheet in the freezer for 30 minutes, before serving up with your beloved strawberries, mouthwatering coconut vanilla ice cream, or decadent chocolate chips.

> This recipe goes well with *The Love Magnet, The Flirty Starters, The Orange Berry Champagne Fairytale*

THE NAUGHTY CHOCOLATE CAKE

SERVES 6
TIME 90 MINUTES   (GF, DF, VEG)

INGREDIENTS

banana
egg
¼ cup coconut creamer
½ cup almond milk, unsweetened
½ cup egg whites
1 cup chocolate cake mix, Simple
    Mills Gluten Free

⅓ cup stevia
½ tbsp baking soda
½ tsp salt
½ cup coconut flour
1 tbsp olive oil

Garnish: **Chopped nuts, coconut flakes, strawberries, and chocolate squares**

DIRECTIONS

1. Preheat the oven to 350 degrees.
2. In a small banana mush the banana up. In a bigger bowl, add one egg and beat until even. Then add egg whites, and mix. Add the banana and mix until even.
3. Add all the wet ingredients including almond milk, coconut creamer, and olive oil to the bowl with the banana and eggs, and mix until even.
4. Add the dry ingredients to wet ingredients and mix until smooth.
5. Then get out a medium circular cake pan. Coat with plant based oil before transferring the batter.
6. Spread the batter evenly and put in the oven for 40 to 45 minutes. Always check the cake with a toothpick to see if it's ready (if the pick comes out clean, with no dough, it's fully cooked).
7. Decorate with strawberries, coconut flakes, and chocolate squares!

This recipe goes well with *The Love Magnet, The Flirty Starters, The Orange Berry Champagne Fairytale, The Mouthwatering Mango Smoothie*

THE ORGASMIC CHOCOLATE COVERED STRAWBERRIES

SERVES   15
TIME   45 MINUTES   (GF, DF, V)

INGREDIENTS

1 package strawberries (19)
10 oz chocolate chips, Vegan
2 tbsp coconut oil
1/2 Cup coconut cream
¼ Cup granola
¼ Cup chopped nuts
Garnish: Coconut whip cream, and coconut vanilla ice cream

DIRECTIONS

1. Wash and dry strawberries well.
2. Get a baking sheet out and prepare with parchment paper.
3. Heat iron skillet with coconut oil to high heat. Then Add chips and as they melt, add coconut cream. Mix evenly.
4. Once the chocolate has melted turn off heat.
5. Have the granola, and chopped nuts ready in individual bowls for dipping. Dip strawberries one by one in melted chocolate. Right after coating the berry with chocolate, dip some in the nuts or granola. Make sure to have individual ones without toppings. Repeat this process with all berries.
6. Let strawberries cool for 10 minutes then place them in the refrigerator for one hour and say bon appetite to mouthwatering moments!

This recipe is the Jackpot in flavor, taste, and love in that it goes with any type of starter, juicy middle, and of course bittersweet ending!

A CHOCOLATE BANANA CAKE FANTASY

SERVES 10
TIME 80 MINUTES   (GF, DF,)

INGREDIENTS

1 ½ cup oat flour
4 egg whites
¼ cup coconut creamer
2 tbsp olive oil
⅓ cup cacao
⅓ cup stevia
bananas mushed

1 tbsp cinnamon
½ tbsp baking powder
¼ tsp salt
½ cup chocolate chips, vegan brand (*Enjoy* brand)
¼ cup nuts

Garnish: Strawberries, coconut vanilla ice cream, chocolate chips, and chocolate candies

DIRECTIONS

1. Preheat oven to 350 degrees Fahrenheit. Next, get out a bundt cake pan for the mixture. Coat the bundt pan with plant based oil and set aside.
2. Add egg whites to a large mixing bowl and beat them.
3. In a small bowl smash bananas with a spoon before adding to bowl with egg whites.
4. Once bananas are smashed with a spoon, add them to the bowl with egg whites. Add 2 tbsp of olive oil, and ¼ cup of coconut creamer. Mix all ingredients until batter is smooth.
5. Add dry ingredients to the wet ingredients, except vegan chocolate chips and nuts.
6. Make sure the mix is blended and all lumps are smoothed out before folding in chocolate chips and nuts. Mix until nuts and chocolate chips are evenly distributed in the batter.
7. Transfer to a bundt cake pan, and spread the batter evenly around the pan.
8. Put cake pan in the oven for 45-50 minutes.
9. After around 45 minutes, check to see if it's done by putting a tooth pick in the center.
10. Oonce it's baked to perfection, remove and let it cool for 25 minutes before serving with strawberries and coconut vanilla ice cream.

> To really make your honey's mouth water serve with any of these recommended recipes: *The Love Magnet, The Flirty Starters, The Orange Berry Champagne Fairytale, The Mouthwatering Mango Smoothie, The Sultry Chocolate Soup*

THE JUICY KISS

A Kiss & Tell Guide to Cooking Up Sexy

STAY TUNED!

This 2019, *The Juicy Kiss, A Kiss & Tell Guide to Cooking Up Sexy*, Volume III in the The Food Orgy™ Series of Books will announce a New Lingo of "Sexy" for all you Gals, in speaking the latest Sexy in fitness, art, fashion, weight loss, dating, spirituality, and more with top articles written by editor Michelle Lynn. Each column will give you the freshest perspective on speaking the language of Sexy along with understanding "The Sexy Recipe" and how to begin to Cook up *The Juicy Kiss* every single day!

THE JUICY KISS
A Kiss & Tell Guide to
Cooking Up Sexy
Editor
Michelle Lynn
VOLUME III IN
THE FOOD ORGY TM
BOOK SERIES

ABOUT *the* AUTHOR

Michelle Lynn is an author, actress, stylist, blogger, self taught chef, and fitness model. She is the founder of THE ZEN FOOD PLAN (zenfoodplan.com) and THE MICHELLE LYNN BRAND (themichellelynnbrand.com). Currently, she has published over 450 of her signature recipes spanning from Instagram, her cookbooks, and ZenFoodPlan website. She drives her artistic inspiration from her everyday surroundings in what she credits to the mindfulness technique called "The Artist Lens," a visual experience that draws upon the present moment of natural surroundings, and experiences.

In her free time you can find her cooking up signature ZenFoodPlan recipes, traveling, practicing yoga, fitness modeling, writing, and taking long runs along the beach. She resides in South Florida, and travels regularly to NYC and Los Angeles for on camera work, writing, modeling, blogging projects, and creative development.